crochet *your cares away*

When life gets stressful, go a little crazy with crochet!

If your computer's bugging you, reformat your mood with an amusing "software" virus. If your diet's a losing battle, let a Hamburger Hat tell the world what you'd rather have for dinner. And since nothing cures the blues like helping others, why not create a cheerful afghan of Smiley Face Blocks for someone who needs a chuckle? We bet you also know a child who would love a game of Tic-Tac-Toast or a zany Snake Scarf to wear.

Designer Meagan Glaser understands that the right attitude can turn a little time with crochet into a stress-buster—no matter what your current project is.

"When you're under pressure," Meagan says, "it can be hard to see anything but the problem at hand. That's why it's important to remember that crochet is your hobby, not your job. If you're making something for someone else, don't worry if you missed a stitch or the finishing is uneven. The main thing they'll see is the time you put into the gift. If you're really struggling with a project, give yourself permission to put it down for a while—or maybe even get rid of it!"

The lighthearted projects in this collection are sure to put you on the road to relaxation!

LEISURE ARTS, INC.
Little Rock, Arkansas

snake scarf

I love snakes and reptiles—I think they're the coolest. Unfortunately, this was seen as odd for a girl when I was twelve. Times are a-changing, so if you're trying to encourage a budding biologist, this might be a nice option. That said, it's also a great scarf for little boys who want something fun—having a snake wrapped around your neck impresses everyone!

—Meagan

EASY

Finished Size: 3"w x $74^{1}/_{2}$"l (7.5 cm x 189 cm)

MATERIALS

Medium Weight Yarn [7 ounces, 364 yards (198 grams, 333 meters) per skein]:
- Green - 1 skein
- Purple - 1 skein
- Yellow and Black - small amount **each**

Crochet hook, size I (5.5 mm) **or** size needed for gauge

Yarn needle

GAUGE: 12 sc and 12 rows = 4" (10 cm)

Gauge Swatch: 4" (10 cm) square
Ch 13.
Row 1: Sc in second ch from hook and in each ch across: 12 sc.
Rows 2-12: Ch 1, turn; sc in each sc across.
Finish off.

STITCH GUIDE

BEGINNING DECREASE

Pull up a loop in first 2 sts, YO and draw through all 3 loops on hook **(counts as one sc)**.

DECREASE

Pull up a loop in next 2 sts, YO and draw through all 3 loops on hook **(counts as one sc)**.

HEAD

With Green, ch 4.

Row 1: Sc in second ch from hook and in each ch across: 3 sc.

Row 2 (Right side)**:** Ch 1, turn; 2 sc in first sc, sc in next sc, 2 sc in last sc: 5 sc.

Note: Loop a short piece of yarn around any stitch to mark Row 2 as **right** side.

Rows 3-5: Ch 1, turn; 2 sc in first sc, sc in each sc across to last sc, 2 sc in last sc: 11 sc.

Row 6: Ch 1, turn; sc in each sc across.

Row 7: Ch 1, turn; 2 sc in first sc, sc in each sc across to last sc, 2 sc in last sc: 13 sc.

Rows 8-13: Ch 1, turn; sc in each sc across.

Row 14 (Decrease row)**:** Ch 1, turn; work beginning decrease, sc in each sc across to last 2 sc, decrease: 11 sc.

Row 15: Ch 1, turn; sc in each sc across.

Rows 16 and 17: Repeat Rows 14 and 15; do **not** finish off: 9 sc.

BODY

Row 1: Ch 1, turn; 2 sc in first sc, sc in each sc across to last 2 sc, decrease.

Row 2: Ch 1, turn; work beginning decrease, sc in each sc across to last sc, 2 sc in last sc.

Rows 3 and 4: Repeat Rows 1 and 2.

Rows 5-8: Ch 1, turn; sc in each sc across.

Finish off.

Row 9: With **right** side facing, join Purple with slip st in first sc; ch 1, pull up a loop in same st and in next sc, YO and draw through all 3 loops on hook **(counts as one sc)**, sc in each sc across to last sc, 2 sc in last sc.

Row 10: Ch 1, turn; 2 sc in first sc, sc in each sc across to last 2 sc, decrease.

Row 11: Ch 1, turn; work beginning decrease, sc in each sc across to last sc, 2 sc in last sc.

Row 12: Ch 1, turn; 2 sc in first sc, sc in each sc across to last 2 sc, decrease.

Rows 13-16: Ch 1, turn; sc in each sc across.

Finish off.

Row 17: With **right** side facing, join Green with sc in first sc *(see Joining With Sc, page 42)*; sc in same st and in each sc across to last 2 sc, decrease.

Rows 18-224: Repeat Rows 2-17, 12 times; then repeat Rows 2-16 once **more**; do **not** finish off.

Instructions continued on page 38.

road scarf

This scarf is for road trips, or mind trips, or those embarking on the rocky roads of Driver's Education. If you want, pick up some cute car- or bus-shaped buttons and sew them along the road.

—Meagan

EASY

Finished Size: 5"w x $66^1/_2$"l (12.5 cm x 169 cm)

MATERIALS

Medium Weight Yarn (MEDIUM 4)
[7 ounces, 364 yards (198 grams, 333 meters) per skein]:
- Black - 1 skein
- White - 40 yards (36.5 meters)
- Yellow - 10 yards (9 meters)

Crochet hook, size I (5.5 mm) **or** size needed for gauge

GAUGE: 12 sc and 12 rows = 4" (10 cm)

Gauge Swatch: 4" (10 cm) square
Ch 13.
Row 1: Sc in second ch from hook and in each ch across: 12 sc.
Rows 2-12: Ch 1, turn; sc in each sc across.
Finish off.

SCARF

With White, ch 200.

Row 1 (Wrong side)**:** Sc in second ch from hook and in each ch across; finish off: 199 sc.

Note: Loop a short piece of yarn around **back** of any stitch on Row 1 to mark **right** side.

Row 2: With **right** side facing, join Black with sc in first sc ***(see Joining With Sc, page 42)***; sc in each sc across.

Rows 3-7: Ch 1, turn; sc in each sc across.

Row 8: Ch 1, turn; sc in first 4 sc changing to Yellow in last sc made ***(Fig. 3a, page 42)***, cut Black, sc in next 4 sc changing to Black in last sc made, cut Yellow, sc in next 4 sc changing to Yellow in last sc made, cut Black, ★ sc in next 4 sc changing to Black in last sc made, cut Yellow, sc in next 4 sc changing to Yellow in last sc made, cut Black; repeat from ★ across to last 3 sc; sc in last 3 sc; finish off.

Row 9: With **wrong** side facing, join Black with sc in first sc; sc in each sc across.

Rows 10-14: Ch 1, turn; sc in each sc across.

Finish off.

Row 15: With **wrong** side facing, join White with sc in first sc; sc in each sc across; finish off.

TIP: Keep a portable project ready so you can crochet in waiting rooms and airports.

pencil scarf

This pencil always reminds me of school days, but it could also remind you of soft pencil sketches or long journal writing sessions. Either way, this is an accessory that not every kid at school will have.

—Meagan

EASY

Finished Size: 4½"w x 78½"l (11.5 cm x 199.5 cm)

MATERIALS

Medium Weight Yarn (MEDIUM 4)
[7 ounces, 364 yards
(198 grams, 333 meters) per skein]:
- Gold - 1 skein
- Black - 40 yards (36.5 meters)
- Grey - 20 yards (18.5 meters)
- Tan and Pink - 10 yards (9.5 meters) **each**

Crochet hook, size I (5.5 mm) **or** size needed for gauge

GAUGE: 12 sc and 12 rows = 4" (10 cm)

Gauge Swatch: 4" (10 cm) square
Ch 13.
Row 1: Sc in second ch from hook and in each ch across: 12 sc.
Rows 2-12: Ch 1, turn; sc in each sc across.
Finish off.

STITCH GUIDE

BEGINNING DECREASE

Pull up a loop in first 2 sts, YO and draw through all 3 loops on hook **(counts as one sc)**.

DECREASE

Pull up a loop in next 2 sts, YO and draw through all 3 loops on hook **(counts as one sc)**.

BODY

With Gold, ch 200.

Row 1 (Right side)**:** Sc in second ch from hook and in each ch across: 199 sc.

Note: Loop a short piece of yarn around any stitch to mark Row 1 as **right** side.

Rows 2 and 3: Ch 1, turn; sc in each sc across.

Finish off.

Row 4: With **wrong** side facing, join Black with sc in first sc *(see Joining With Sc, page 42)*; sc in each sc across; finish off.

Row 5: With **right** side facing, join Gold with sc in first sc; sc in each sc across.

Rows 6-9: Ch 1, turn; sc in each sc across.

Finish off.

Row 10: With **wrong** side facing, join Black with sc in first sc; sc in each sc across; finish off.

Row 11: With **right** side facing, join Gold with sc in first sc; sc in each sc across.

Rows 12 and 13: Ch 1, turn; sc in each sc across.

Finish off.

FERRULE

Row 1: With **right** side of either short end facing and working in end of rows, join Grey with sc in first row; sc in each row across: 13 sc.

Rows 2-15: Ch 1, turn; sc in each sc across.

Finish off.

ERASER

Row 1: With **wrong** side facing, join Pink with sc in first sc on Ferrule; sc in each sc across.

Rows 2-5: Ch 1, turn; sc in each sc across.

Rows 6 and 7: Ch 1, turn; work beginning decrease, sc in each sc across to last 2 sc, decrease: 9 sc.

Finish off.

PENCIL TIP

Row 1: With **wrong** side of remaining short end facing and working in end of rows, join Tan with sc in first row; sc in each row across: 13 sc.

Row 2: Ch 1, turn; sc in each sc across.

Row 3 (Decrease row)**:** Ch 1, turn; work beginning decrease, sc in each sc across to last 2 sc, decrease: 11 sc.

Rows 4-10: Repeat Rows 2 and 3, 3 times; then repeat Row 2 once **more**: 5 sc.

Row 11: Ch 1, turn; work beginning decrease, sc in next sc, decrease; finish off: 3 sc.

Row 12: With **right** side facing, join Black with sc in first sc; sc in last 2 sc.

Row 13: Ch 1, turn; work beginning decrease, sc in last sc: 2 sc.

Row 14: Ch 1, turn; decrease; finish off.

diamond illusion scarf

This is one of the first scarves I ever "designed." I was fascinated by the idea of revealing an image in contrasting color patterns. I basically wanted an image that gave the effect of illusion knitting, but without having to move the piece to see an image pop out. I did get dizzy looking at this once, though.

—Meagan

EASY

Finished Size: 6½"w x 56"l
(16.5 cm x 142 cm)

MATERIALS

Medium Weight Yarn (MEDIUM 4)
[7 ounces, 364 yards
(198 grams, 333 meters) per skein]:
Black - 1 skein
White - 1 skein

Crochet hook, size I (5.5 mm) **or** size needed for gauge

GAUGE: In pattern, 12 sc = 4" (10 cm);
10 rows = 3½" (9 cm)

Gauge Swatch: 4" (10 cm) square
Ch 13.
Row 1: Sc in second ch from hook and in each ch across: 12 sc.
Rows 2-12: Ch 1, turn; sc in each sc across.
Finish off.

SCARF

With Black, ch 20.

Row 1 (Right side)**:** Sc in second ch from hook and in each ch across: 19 sc.

Note: Loop a short piece of yarn around any stitch to mark Row 1 as **right** side.

Row 2: Ch 1, turn; sc in first 8 sc changing to White in last sc made ***(Fig. 3b, page 42)***, do **not** cut Black, working over Black, sc in next 3 sc changing to Black, do **not** cut White, working over White, sc in last 8 sc changing to White.

Continue to change color in same manner throughout, working over color not being used.

Row 3: Ch 1, turn; sc in first 7 sc, with Black sc in next 5 sc, with White sc in last 7 sc.

Row 4: Ch 1, turn; sc in first 6 sc, with Black sc in next 7 sc, with White sc in last 6 sc.

Row 5: With Black, ch 1, turn; sc in first 5 sc, with White sc in next 9 sc, with Black sc in last 5 sc.

Row 6: Ch 1, turn; sc in first 4 sc, with White sc in next 11 sc, with Black sc in last 4 sc.

Row 7: With White, ch 1, turn; sc in first 3 sc, with Black sc in next 13 sc, with White sc in last 3 sc.

Row 8: Ch 1, turn; sc in first 3 sc, with Black sc in next 13 sc, with White sc in last 3 sc.

Row 9: With Black, ch 1, turn; sc in first 3 sc, with White sc in next 13 sc, with Black sc in last 3 sc.

Row 10: Ch 1, turn; sc in first 4 sc, with White sc in next 11 sc, with Black sc in last 4 sc.

Row 11: With White, ch 1, turn; sc in first 5 sc, with Black sc in next 9 sc, with White sc in last 5 sc.

Row 12: Ch 1, turn; sc in first 6 sc, with Black sc in next 7 sc, with White sc in last 6 sc.

Row 13: With Black, ch 1, turn; sc in first 7 sc, with White sc in next 5 sc, with Black sc in last 7 sc.

Row 14: Ch 1, turn; sc in first 8 sc, with White sc in next 3 sc, with Black sc in last 8 sc.

Row 15: With White, ch 1, turn; sc in each sc across.

Row 16: Ch 1, turn; sc in first 8 sc, with Black sc in next 3 sc, with White sc in last 8 sc.

Row 17: With Black, ch 1, turn; sc in first 7 sc, with White sc in next 5 sc, with Black sc in last 7 sc.

Row 18: Ch 1, turn; sc in first 6 sc, with White sc in next 7 sc, with Black sc in last 6 sc.

Row 19: With White, ch 1, turn; sc in first 5 sc, with Black sc in next 9 sc, with White sc in last 5 sc.

Row 20: Ch 1, turn; sc in first 4 sc, with Black sc in next 11 sc, with White sc in last 4 sc.

Row 21: With Black, ch 1, turn; sc in first 3 sc, with White sc in next 13 sc, with Black sc in last 3 sc.

Row 22: Ch 1, turn; sc in first 3 sc, with White sc in next 13 sc, with Black sc in last 3 sc.

Row 23: With White, ch 1, turn; sc in first 3 sc, with Black sc in next 13 sc, with White sc in last 3 sc.

Row 24: Ch 1, turn; sc in first 4 sc, with Black sc in next 11 sc, with White sc in last 4 sc.

Row 25: With Black, ch 1, turn; sc in first 5 sc, with White sc in next 9 sc, with Black sc in last 5 sc.

Row 26: Ch 1, turn; sc in first 6 sc, with White sc in next 7 sc, with Black sc in last 6 sc.

Row 27: With White, ch 1, turn; sc in first 7 sc, with Black sc in next 5 sc, with White sc in last 7 sc.

Row 28: Ch 1, turn; sc in first 8 sc, with Black sc in next 3 sc, with White sc in last 8 sc.

Row 29: With Black, ch 1, turn; sc in each sc across.

Rows 30-169: Repeat Rows 2-29, 5 times.

Finish off.

tic-tac-toast

Finally, food that exists solely to be played with! —*Meagan*

EASY

Finished Size: 17"w x 14"h (43 cm x 35.5 cm)

MATERIALS

MEDIUM 4

Medium Weight Yarn
[7 ounces, 364 yards
(198 grams, 333 meters) per skein]:
White - 1 skein
Tan - 25 yards (23 meters)
Dk Red - 20 yards (18.5 meters)
Yellow - 5 yards (4.5 meters)
Red - small amount
Crochet hook, size J (6 mm) **or** size needed for gauge
Yarn needle

GAUGE: 11 sc and 14 rows = 4" (10 cm)

Gauge Swatch: 4" (10 cm) square
Ch 12.
Row 1: Sc in second ch from hook and in each ch across: 11 sc.
Rows 2-14: Ch 1, turn; sc in each sc across.
Finish off.

STITCH GUIDE

BEGINNING DECREASE

Pull up a loop in first 2 sts, YO and draw through all 3 loops on hook **(counts as one sc)**.

DECREASE

Pull up a loop in next 2 sts, YO and draw through all 3 loops on hook **(counts as one sc)**.

BACON STRIP (Make 4)

With Dk Red, ch 41.

Row 1: Sc in second ch from hook and in each ch across: 40 sc.

Row 2 (Right side)**:** Ch 1, turn; sc in each sc across; finish off.

Note: Loop a short piece of yarn around any stitch to mark Row 2 as **right** side.

Row 3: With **wrong** side facing, join White with sc in first sc *(see Joining With Sc, page 42)*; sc in each sc across; finish off.

Row 4: With **right** side facing, join Dk Red with sc in first sc; sc in each sc across.

Row 5: Ch 1, turn; sc in each sc across; finish off.

Row 6: With **right** side facing, join White with sc in first sc; sc in each sc across; finish off.

FRIED EGG (Make 10)

Rnd 1 (Wrong side)**:** With Yellow, ch 2; 6 sc in second ch from hook; join with slip st to first sc.

Note: Mark **back** of any stitch on Rnd 1 as **right** side.

Rnd 2: Ch 1, 2 sc in same st and in each sc around; join with slip st to first sc, finish off: 12 sc.

Rnd 3: With **wrong** side facing, join White with sc in same st; sc in same st and in next sc, (2 sc in next sc, sc in next sc) around; join with slip st to first sc: 18 sc.

Rnd 4: Ch 1, 2 sc in same st, sc in next 2 sc, (2 sc in next sc, sc in next 2 sc) around; join with slip st to first sc: 24 sc.

Rnd 5: Ch 1, skip first sc, sc in next 15 sc, slip st in next sc, leave remaining 7 sts unworked; finish off.

Using photo as a guide, with **right** side facing and Red, add straight stitch X to five Eggs *(Fig. 5, page 43)*.

TOAST

BODY

With Tan, ch 45.

Row 1 (Wrong side)**:** Sc in second ch from hook and in each ch across: 44 sc.

Note: Mark **back** of any stitch on Row 1 as **right** side.

Rows 2-42: Ch 1, turn; sc in each sc across.

Rows 43-45: Ch 1, turn; 2 sc in first sc, sc in each sc across to last sc, 2 sc in last sc: 50 sc.

Row 46: Ch 1, turn; sc in each sc across.

Rows 47-49: Ch 1, turn; work beginning decrease, sc in each sc across to last 2 sc, decrease: 44 sc.

Finish off.

CRUST

Rnd 1: With **right** side facing, join Tan with sc in first sc on Row 49; sc in each sc across; sc in end of each row across; working in free loops of beginning ch *(Fig. 2, page 42)*, 3 sc in ch at base of first sc, sc in each ch across to last ch, 3 sc in last ch; sc in end of each row across; join with slip st to first sc.

Rnd 2: Ch 1, ★ sc in each sc across to center sc of next 3-sc group, 3 sc in center sc; repeat from ★ once **more**, sc in each sc across; join with slip st to first sc, finish off.

Using photo as a guide and White, sew Bacon Strip across Row 6 to Toast to form crossed lines.

afghan squares

Someone you know would love to have their own Smiley Face, Peace Sign, or Yin-Yang (harmony) "comfort-ghans."

—Meagan

smiley face

EASY

Finished Size: 6¼" (16 cm) square

MATERIALS

Medium Weight Yarn (MEDIUM 4)
[7 ounces, 364 yards
(198 grams, 333 meters) per skein]:
Yellow - 25 yards (23 meters)
Black - 15 yards (13.5 meters) skein
Crochet hook, size I (5.5 mm) **or** size needed for gauge
Yarn needle

GAUGE: Each Square = 6¼" (16 cm)

Gauge Swatch: 4" (10 cm) diameter
Work Rnds 1-6 of Square.

STITCH GUIDE

TREBLE CROCHET *(abbreviated tr)*
YO twice, insert hook in st indicated, YO and pull up a loop (4 loops on hook), (YO and draw through 2 loops on hook) 3 times.

SQUARE

Rnd 1 (Wrong side)**:** With Yellow, ch 2; 6 sc in second ch from hook; join with slip st to first sc.

Note: Loop a short piece of yarn around **back** of any stitch on Rnd 1 to mark **right** side.

Rnd 2: Ch 1, 2 sc in each sc around; join with slip st to first sc: 12 sc.

Rnd 3: Ch 1, 2 sc in same st, sc in next sc, (2 sc in next sc, sc in next sc) around; join with slip st to first sc: 18 sc.

Rnd 4: Ch 1, 2 sc in same st, sc in next 2 sc, (2 sc in next sc, sc in next 2 sc) around; join with slip st to first sc: 24 sc.

Rnd 5: Ch 1, 2 sc in same st, sc in next 3 sc, (2 sc in next sc, sc in next 3 sc) around; join with slip st to first sc: 30 sc.

Rnd 6: Ch 1, 2 sc in same st, sc in next 4 sc, (2 sc in next sc, sc in next 4 sc) around; join with slip st to first sc: 36 sc.

Rnd 7: Ch 1, 2 sc in same st, sc in next 5 sc, (2 sc in next sc, sc in next 5 sc) around; join with slip st to first sc: 42 sc.

Rnd 8: Ch 1, 2 sc in same st, sc in next 6 sc, (2 sc in next sc, sc in next 6 sc) around; join with slip st to first sc, finish off: 48 sc.

Rnd 9: With **wrong** side facing, join Black with sc in same st as joining *(see Joining With Sc, page 42)*; sc in next 2 sc, ★ † hdc in next sc, dc in next sc, tr in next sc, 3 tr in next sc, dc in next sc, hdc in next sc †, sc in next 6 sc; repeat from ★ 2 times **more**, then repeat from † to † once, sc in last 3 sc; join with slip st to first sc, finish off: 56 sts.

Rnd 10: With **wrong** side facing, join Yellow with sc in same st as joining; sc in next 5 sts, 2 sc in each of next 2 sts, (sc in next 12 sts, 2 sc in each of next 2 sts) 3 times, sc in last 6 sts; join with slip st to first sc; finish off: 64 sc.

Using photo as a guide, with **right** side facing and 2 strands of Black, add straight stitch smiley face *(Fig. 5, page 43)*.

peace sign

EASY

Finished Size: 6¼" (16 cm) square

MATERIALS
- Medium Weight Yarn (MEDIUM 4)
  - [7 ounces, 364 yards (198 grams, 333 meters) per skein]:
    - White - 25 yards (23 meters)
    - Black - 20 yards (18.5 meters)
- Crochet hook, size I (5.5 mm) **or** size needed for gauge
- Yarn needle

GAUGE: Each Square = 6¼" (16 cm)

Gauge Swatch: 4" (10 cm) diameter
Work Rnds 1-6 of Square.

STITCH GUIDE

TREBLE CROCHET *(abbreviated tr)*
YO twice, insert hook in st indicated, YO and pull up a loop (4 loops on hook), (YO and draw through 2 loops on hook) 3 times.

SQUARE

Rnd 1 (Right side)**:** With White, ch 2, 6 sc in second ch from hook; join with slip st to first sc.

Note: Loop a short piece of yarn around **back** of any stitch on Rnd 1 to mark as **right** side.

Rnd 2: Ch 1, 2 sc in each sc around; join with slip st to first sc: 12 sc.

Rnd 3: Ch 1, 2 sc in same st, sc in next sc, (2 sc in next sc, sc in next sc) around; join with slip st to first sc: 18 sc.

Rnd 4: Ch 1, 2 sc in same st, sc in next 2 sc, (2 sc in next sc, sc in next 2 sc) around; join with slip st to first sc: 24 sc.

Rnd 5: Ch 1, 2 sc in same st, sc in next 3 sc, (2 sc in next sc, sc in next 3 sc) around; join with slip st to first sc: 30 sc.

Rnd 6: Ch 1, 2 sc in same st, sc in next 4 sc, (2 sc in next sc, sc in next 4 sc) around; join with slip st to first sc: 36 sc.

Rnd 7: Ch 1, 2 sc in same st, sc in next 5 sc, (2 sc in next sc, sc in next 5 sc) around; join with slip st to first sc: 42 sc.

Rnd 8: Ch 1, 2 sc in same st, sc in next 6 sc, (2 sc in next sc, sc in next 6 sc) around; join with slip st to first sc, finish off: 48 sc.

Rnd 9: With **wrong** side facing, join Black with sc in same st as joining ***(see Joining With Sc, page 42)***; sc in next 2 sc, ★ † hdc in next sc, dc in next sc, tr in next sc, 3 tr in next sc, dc in next sc, hdc in next sc †, sc in next 6 sc; repeat from ★ 2 times **more**, then repeat from † to † once, sc in last 3 sc; join with slip st to first sc, finish off: 56 sts.

Rnd 10: Ch 1, sc in same st and in next 5 sts, 2 sc in each of next 2 sts, (sc in next 12 sts, 2 sc in each of next 2 sts) 3 times, sc in last 6 sts; join with slip st to first sc; finish off: 64 sc.

Using photo as a guide, with **right** side facing and 2 strands of Black, add straight stitch peace sign *(Fig. 5, page 43)*.

yin-yang

EASY

Finished Size: 6¼" (16 cm) square

MATERIALS
- Medium Weight Yarn (MEDIUM 4)
  - [7 ounces, 364 yards (198 grams, 333 meters) per skein]:
    - White - 45 yards (41 meters)
    - Black - 45 yards (41 meters)
- Crochet hook, size I (5.5 mm) **or** size needed for gauge
- Yarn needle

GAUGE: Each Square = $6^1/_4$" (16 cm)

Gauge Swatch: 4" (10 cm) diameter
Work Rnds 1-6 of Square.

STITCH GUIDE

TREBLE CROCHET *(abbreviated tr)*
YO twice, insert hook in st indicated, YO and pull up a loop (4 loops on hook), (YO and draw through 2 loops on hook) 3 times.

SQUARE

Rnd 1 (Right side)**:** With White, ch 2, 3 sc in second ch from hook changing to Black *(Fig. 3b, page 42)*, working over White, do **not** cut White, 3 sc in same ch; join with slip st to first sc.

Note: Loop a short piece of yarn around back of any stitch on Rnd 1 to mark as **right** side.

Continue to change color in same manner throughout, working over color not being used.

Rnd 2: With White, ch 1, 2 sc in each of next 3 sc, with Black 2 sc in each of last 3 sc; join with slip st to first sc: 12 sc.

Rnd 3: With White, ch 1, 2 sc in same st, sc in next sc, (2 sc in next sc, sc in next sc) twice, with Black, (2 sc in next sc, sc in next sc) 3 times; join with slip st to first sc: 18 sc.

Rnd 4: With White, ch 1, 2 sc in same st, sc in next 2 sc, (2 sc in next sc, sc in next 2 sc) twice, with Black, (2 sc in next sc, sc in next 2 sc) 3 times; join with slip st to first sc: 24 sc.

Rnd 5: With White, ch 1, 2 sc in same st, sc in next 3 sc, (2 sc in next sc, sc in next 3 sc) twice, with Black, (2 sc in next sc, sc in next 3 sc) 3 times; join with slip st to first sc: 30 sc.

Rnd 6: With White, ch 1, 2 sc in same st, sc in next 4 sc, (2 sc in next sc, sc in next 4 sc) twice, with Black, (2 sc in next sc, sc in next 4 sc) 3 times; join with slip st to first sc: 36 sc.

Rnd 7: With White, ch 1, 2 sc in same st, sc in next 5 sc, (2 sc in next sc, sc in next 5 sc) twice, with Black, (2 sc in next sc, sc in next 5 sc) 3 times; join with slip st to first sc: 42 sc.

Rnd 8: With White, ch 1, 2 sc in same st, sc in next 6 sc, (2 sc in next sc, sc in next 6 sc) twice, with Black, (2 sc in next sc, sc in next 6 sc) 3 times; join with slip st to first sc: 48 sc.

Rnd 9: With Black, ch 1, sc in same st and in next 2 sc, ♥ † hdc in next sc, dc in next sc, tr in next sc, 3 tr in next sc, dc in next sc, hdc in next sc †, sc in next 6 sc; repeat from † to † once ♥; sc in next 3 sc, with White, sc in next 3 sc, repeat from ♥ to ♥ once, sc in last 3 sc; join with slip st to first sc, finish off White only: 56 sts.

Rnd 10: With Black, ch 1, sc in same st and in next 5 sts, 2 sc in each of next 2 sts, sc in next 12 sts, 2 sc in each of next 2 sts, sc in next 6 sts, cut Black; with White, sc in next 6 sts, 2 sc in each of next 2 sts, sc in next 12 sts, 2 sc in each of next 2 sts, sc in last 6 sts; join with slip st to first sc, finish off: 64 sc.

DOT (Make one each in Black and White)

Rnd 1 (Right side)**:** Ch 2, 6 sc in second ch from hook; join with slip st to first sc, finish off leaving a long end for sewing.

Note: Mark **back** of any stitch on Rnd 1 as **right** side.

Using photo as a guide, with **right** side facing, sew Dots to Square.

OPTIONAL AFGHAN SIZES

For a child size afghan - finished measurement of $37^1/_2$" x 50" (95.5 cm x 127 cm); you will need 48 squares; whipstitch the squares together having 6 squares by 8 squares to complete the afghan *(Fig. 4, page 43)*.

For a full size afghan - finished measurement of 50" x 69" (127 cm x 175.5 cm); you will need 88 squares; whipstitch the squares together having 8 squares by 11 squares to complete the afghan *(Fig. 4, page 43)*.

traffic light pillow

For home décor that's a little "racy."

—Meagan

Finished Size: $6^{1}/_{4}$"w x $18^{3}/_{4}$"h (16 cm x 47.5 cm)

MATERIALS

Medium Weight Yarn (MEDIUM 4)
[7 ounces, 364 yards
(198 grams, 333 meters) per skein]:
Black - 1 skein
Red - 25 yards (23 meters)
Yellow - 25 yards (23 meters)
Green - 25 yards (23 meters)
Crochet hook, size I (5.5 mm) **or** size needed for gauge
Polyester fiberfill
Yarn needle

GAUGE: Each Square = $6^{1}/_{4}$" (16 cm)

Gauge Swatch: 4" (10 cm) diameter
Work Rnds 1-6 of Light.

STITCH GUIDE

TREBLE CROCHET *(abbreviated tr)*
YO twice, insert hook in st indicated, YO and pull up a loop (4 loops on hook), (YO and draw through 2 loops on hook) 3 times.

FRONT

LIGHT (Make one each in Red, Yellow, and Green)

Rnd 1 (Wrong side)**:** Ch 2, 6 sc in second ch from hook; join with slip st to first sc.

Note: Loop a short piece of yarn around **back** of any stitch on Rnd 1 to mark **right** side.

Rnd 2: Ch 1, 2 sc in each sc around; join with slip st to first sc: 12 sc.

Rnd 3: Ch 1, 2 sc in same st, sc in next sc, (2 sc in next sc, sc in next sc) around; join with slip st to first sc: 18 sc.

Rnd 4: Ch 1, 2 sc in same st, sc in next 2 sc, (2 sc in next sc, sc in next 2 sc) around; join with slip st to first sc: 24 sc.

Rnd 5: Ch 1, 2 sc in same st, sc in next 3 sc, (2 sc in next sc, sc in next 3 sc) around; join with slip st to first sc: 30 sc.

Rnd 6: Ch 1, 2 sc in same st, sc in next 4 sc, (2 sc in next sc, sc in next 4 sc) around; join with slip st to first sc: 36 sc.

Rnd 7: Ch 1, 2 sc in same st, sc in next 5 sc, (2 sc in next sc, sc in next 5 sc) around; join with slip st to first sc: 42 sc.

Rnd 8: Ch 1, 2 sc in same st, sc in next 6 sc, (2 sc in next sc, sc in next 6 sc) around; join with slip st to first sc, finish off: 48 sc.

BORDER

Rnd 1: With **wrong** side facing, join Black with sc in any sc *(see Joining With Sc, page 42)*; sc in next 5 sc, hdc in next sc, dc in next sc, tr in next sc, 3 tr in next sc, dc in next sc, hdc in next sc, ★ sc in next 6 sc, hdc in next sc, dc in next sc, tr in next sc, 3 tr in next sc, dc in next sc, hdc in next sc; repeat from ★ 2 times **more**; join with slip st to first sc: 56 sts.

Rnd 2: Ch 1, sc in first 10 sts, 3 sc in next tr, ★ sc in next 13 sts, 3 sc in next tr; repeat from ★ 2 times **more**, sc in last 3 sts; join with slip st to first sc, finish off: 64 sts.

BACK

With Black, ch 17.

Row 1 (Wrong side)**:** Sc in second ch from hook and in each ch across: 16 sc.

Note: Mark **back** of any stitch on Rnd 1 as **right** side.

Rows 2-59: Ch 1, turn; sc in each sc across.

Finish off.

ASSEMBLY

With Black and working in **both** loops, whipstitch Red and Green Lights to opposite ends of Yellow Light *(Fig. 4, page 43)*, forming one vertical Strip of 3 Lights, beginning in center tr of one corner 3-tr group and ending in center tr of next corner 3-tr group.

With **wrong** sides of Front and Back together and working through **both** thicknesses, join Black with slip st in top left corner; slip st evenly around 3 sides, stuff with polyester fiberfill, slip st across remaining side; join with slip st to first slip st, finish off.

beaker pillow

The only experimenting I ever did was with yarn, but I love the "geekyness" of this beaker pillow. Make it for a science teacher, a chemistry-set wielding friend, or for the room of a child who's tired of baby dolls or model airplanes. One side is worked to look partially full, the other side is worked to look empty, so you can "pour out" the contents.

—Meagan

EASY

Finished Size: 12"w (widest part) x 12½"h (30.5 cm x 32 cm)

MATERIALS

Medium Weight Yarn (MEDIUM 4)
[7 ounces, 364 yards (198 grams, 333 meters) per skein]:
Grey - 75 yards (68.5 meters)
Green - 40 yards (36.5 meters)
Crochet hook, size K (6.5 mm) **or** size needed for gauge
Polyester fiberfill
Yarn needle

GAUGE: 10 sc and 11 rows = 4" (10 cm)

Gauge Swatch: 4" (10 cm) square
Ch 11.
Row 1: Sc in second ch from hook and in each ch across: 10 sc.
Rows 2-11: Ch 1, turn; sc in each sc across.
Finish off.

STITCH GUIDE

BEGINNING DECREASE

Pull up a loop in first 2 sts, YO and draw through all 3 loops on hook **(counts as one sc)**.

DECREASE

Pull up a loop in next 2 sts, YO and draw through all 3 loops on hook **(counts as one sc)**.

EMPTY SIDE

With Grey, ch 11.

Row 1: Sc in second ch from hook and in each ch across: 10 sc.

Row 2 (Right side)**:** Ch 1, turn; sc in each sc across.

Note: Loop a short piece of yarn around any stitch to mark Row 2 as **right** side.

Row 3: Ch 1, turn; work beginning decrease, sc in each sc across to last 2 sc, decrease: 8 sc.

Rows 4-12: Ch 1, turn; sc in each sc across.

Row 13 (Increase row)**:** Ch 1, turn; 2 sc in first sc, sc in each sc across to last sc, 2 sc in last sc: 10 sc.

Row 14: Ch 1, turn; sc in each sc across.

Rows 15-34: Repeat Rows 13 and 14, 10 times: 30 sc.

Finish off.

PARTIALLY FULL SIDE

Work same as Empty Side through Row 20; at end of Row 20, finish off: 16 sc.

Row 21: With **wrong** side facing, join Green with sc in first sc *(see Joining With Sc, page 42)*; sc in same st, sc in each sc across to last sc, 2 sc in last sc: 18 sc.

Row 22: Ch 1, turn; sc in each sc across.

Rows 23-34: Repeat Rows 13 and 14, 6 times: 30 sc.

Finish off.

With **wrong** sides of Empty Side and Partially Full Side together, sew together stuff with polyester fiberfill before closing.

TIP: Have projects of different sizes and styles so you can switch between them to suit your mood.

fortune cookie pillow

I always thought that the shape of fortune cookies would make an excellent neck pillow, if only they were large and soft. Voilá!

—Meagan

EASY

Finished Size: 10¼"w x 5"h (26 cm x 12.5 cm)

MATERIALS

MEDIUM 4

Medium Weight Yarn
- [7 ounces, 364 yards (198 grams, 333 meters) per skein]:
  - Tan - 1 skein
  - White - 10 yards (9.5 meters)

Crochet hook, size I (5.5 mm) **or** size needed for gauge
Polyester fiberfill
Yarn needle

GAUGE SWATCH: 4" (10 cm) diameter
Work Rnds 1-6 of Cookie.

COOKIE

Rnd 1 (Wrong side)**:** With Tan, ch 2, 6 sc in second ch from hook; join with slip st to first sc.

Note: Loop a short piece of yarn around **back** of any stitch on Rnd 1 to mark **right** side.

Rnd 2: Ch 1, 2 sc in each sc around; join with slip st to first sc: 12 sc.

Rnd 3: Ch 1, 2 sc in same st, sc in next sc, (2 sc in next sc, sc in next sc) around; join with slip st to first sc: 18 sc.

Rnd 4: Ch 1, 2 sc in same st, sc in next 2 sc, (2 sc in next sc, sc in next 2 sc) around; join with slip st to first sc: 24 sc.

Rnd 5: Ch 1, 2 sc in same st, sc in next 3 sc, (2 sc in next sc, sc in next 3 sc) around; join with slip st to first sc: 30 sc.

Rnd 6: Ch 1, 2 sc in same st, sc in next 4 sc, (2 sc in next sc, sc in next 4 sc) around; join with slip st to first sc: 36 sc.

Rnd 7: Ch 1, 2 sc in same st, sc in next 5 sc, (2 sc in next sc, sc in next 5 sc) around; join with slip st to first sc: 42 sc.

Rnd 8: Ch 1, 2 sc in same st, sc in next 6 sc, (2 sc in next sc, sc in next 6 sc) around; join with slip st to first sc: 48 sc.

Rnd 9: Ch 1, 2 sc in same st, sc in next 7 sc, (2 sc in next sc, sc in next 7 sc) around; join with slip st to first sc: 54 sc.

Rnd 10: Ch 1, 2 sc in same st, sc in next 8 sc, (2 sc in next sc, sc in next 8 sc) around; join with slip st to first sc: 60 sc.

Rnd 11: Ch 1, 2 sc in same st, sc in next 9 sc, (2 sc in next sc, sc in next 9 sc) around; join with slip st to first sc: 66 sc.

Rnd 12: Ch 1, 2 sc in same st, sc in next 10 sc, (2 sc in next sc, sc in next 10 sc) around; join with slip st to first sc: 72 sc.

Rnd 13: Ch 1, 2 sc in same st, sc in next 11 sc, (2 sc in next sc, sc in next 11 sc) around; join with slip st to first sc: 78 sc.

Rnd 14: Ch 1, 2 sc in same st, sc in next 12 sc, (2 sc in next sc, sc in next 12 sc) around; join with slip st to first sc: 84 sc.

Rnd 15: Ch 1, 2 sc in same st, sc in next 13 sc, (2 sc in next sc, sc in next 13 sc) around; join with slip st to first sc: 90 sc.

Rnd 16: Ch 1, 2 sc in same st, sc in next 14 sc, (2 sc in next sc, sc in next 14 sc) around; join with slip st to first sc: 96 sc.

Rnd 17: Ch 1, 2 sc in same st, sc in next 15 sc, (2 sc in next sc, sc in next 15 sc) around; join with slip st to first sc: 102 sc.

Rnd 18: Ch 1, 2 sc in same st, sc in next 16 sc, (2 sc in next sc, sc in next 16 sc) around; join with slip st to first sc: 108 sc.

Rnd 19: Ch 1, 2 sc in same st, sc in next 17 sc, (2 sc in next sc, sc in next 17 sc) around; join with slip st to first sc: 114 sc.

Rnd 20: Ch 1, 2 sc in same st, sc in next 18 sc, (2 sc in next sc, sc in next 18 sc) around; join with slip st to first sc: 120 sc.

Rnd 21: Ch 1, 2 sc in same st, sc in next 19 sc, (2 sc in next sc, sc in next 19 sc) around; join with slip st to first sc: 126 sc.

Rnd 22: Ch 1, 2 sc in same st, sc in next 20 sc, (2 sc in next sc, sc in next 20 sc) around; join with slip st to first sc, finish off leaving a long end for sewing: 132 sc.

FORTUNE (Make 2)

With White, ch 11.

Row 1 (Right side)**:** Sc in second ch from hook and in each ch across: 10 sc.

Note: Mark Row 1 as **right** side.

Rows 2 and 3: Ch 1, turn; sc in each sc across.

Finish off.

FINISHING

Fold Cookie in half with **wrong** side together and joining at one side. Thread yarn needle with long end and whipstitch last rnd together *(Fig. 4, page 43)*. stuffing before closing.
Using photo as a guide and White, Fold Fortune in half lengthwise, sew one Fortune to each end along seam.
Using photo as a guide and Tan, tack center of Cookie to form bend.

moody pillow

Want to warn the world of your mood? Flip the pillow over to advertise when you need a hug, or when you are willing to give 'em out.

—Meagan

EASY

Finished Size: 8½" (21.5 cm) diameter

MATERIALS

MEDIUM 4

Medium Weight Yarn
[7 ounces, 364 yards (198 grams, 333 meters) per skein]:
- Yellow - 65 yards (59.5 meters)
- Blue - 65 yards (59.5 meters)
- Black - 10 yards (9 meters)

Crochet hook, size I (5.5 mm) **or** size needed for gauge
Polyester fiberfill
Yarn needle

GAUGE SWATCH: 4" (10 cm) diameter
Work Rnds 1-6 of Happy Side.

HAPPY SIDE

Rnd 1 (Wrong side)**:** With Yellow, ch 2, 6 sc in second ch from hook; join with slip st to first sc.

Note: Loop a short piece of yarn around **back** of any stitch on Rnd 1 to mark **right** side.

Rnd 2: Ch 1, 2 sc in each sc around; join with slip st to first sc: 12 sc.

Rnd 3: Ch 1, 2 sc in same st, sc in next sc, (2 sc in next sc, sc in next sc) around; join with slip st to first sc: 18 sc.

Rnd 4: Ch 1, 2 sc in same st, sc in next 2 sc, (2 sc in next sc, sc in next 2 sc) around; join with slip st to first sc: 24 sc.

Rnd 5: Ch 1, 2 sc in same st, sc in next 3 sc, (2 sc in next sc, sc in next 3 sc) around; join with slip st to first sc: 30 sc.

Rnd 6: Ch 1, 2 sc in same st, sc in next 4 sc, (2 sc in next sc, sc in next 4 sc) around; join with slip st to first sc: 36 sc.

Rnd 7: Ch 1, 2 sc in same st, sc in next 5 sc, (2 sc in next sc, sc in next 5 sc) around; join with slip st to first sc: 42 sc.

Rnd 8: Ch 1, 2 sc in same st, sc in next 6 sc, (2 sc in next sc, sc in next 6 sc) around; join with slip st to first sc: 48 sc.

Rnd 9: Ch 1, 2 sc in same st, sc in next 7 sc, (2 sc in next sc, sc in next 7 sc) around; join with slip st to first sc: 54 sc.

Rnd 10: Ch 1, 2 sc in same st, sc in next 8 sc, (2 sc in next sc, sc in next 8 sc) around; join with slip st to first sc: 60 sc.

Rnd 11: Ch 1, 2 sc in same st, sc in next 9 sc, (2 sc in next sc, sc in next 9 sc) around; join with slip st to first sc: 66 sc.

Rnd 12: Ch 1, 2 sc in same st, sc in next 10 sc, (2 sc in next sc, sc in next 10 sc) around; join with slip st to first sc: 72 sc.

Rnd 13: Ch 1, 2 sc in same st, sc in next 11 sc, (2 sc in next sc, sc in next 11 sc) around; join with slip st to first sc: 78 sc.

Rnd 14: Ch 1, 2 sc in same st, sc in next 12 sc, (2 sc in next sc, sc in next 12 sc) around; join with slip st to first sc, finish off: 84 sc.

SAD SIDE

With Blue, work same as Happy Side.

EYE (Make 4)

Rnd 1 (Wrong side)**:** With Black, ch 2, 6 sc in second ch from hook; join with slip st to first sc.

Note: Mark **back** of any stitch on Rnd 1 as **right** side.

Rnd 2: Ch 1, 2 sc in each sc around; join with slip st to first sc, finish off: 12 sc.

MOUTH (Make 2)

With Black, ch 20.

Row 1 (Right side)**:** Sc in second ch from hook and in each ch across, finish off: 19 sc.

Note: Mark Row 1 as **right** side.

FINISHING

Using photo as a guide, sew two Eyes to each side. Sew one Mouth with a smile on the Happy Side. Sew remaining Mouth with a frown to the Sad Side.

With **wrong** sides of both pieces together, Happy Side facing, and working through **both** loops on **both** pieces, join Yellow with slip st in any sc; slip st in each sc around stuffing with polyester fiberfill before closing; join with slip st to first slip st, finish off.

pie pillow

May I present the only pie in the world that can be used in a pie fight and not result in hours of cleanup!

—Meagan

EASY

Finished Size: 10" (25.5 cm) diameter

MATERIALS

Medium Weight Yarn (MEDIUM 4)
[7 ounces, 364 yards (198 grams, 333 meters) per skein]:
- Gold - 1 skein
- Red - 75 yards (68.5 meters)

Crochet hook, size I (5.5 mm) **or** size needed for gauge
Polyester fiberfill

GAUGE SWATCH: 4" (10 cm) diameter
Work Rnds 1-6 of Crust.

BOTTOM CRUST

Rnd 1 (Wrong side)**:** With Gold, ch 2, 6 sc in second ch from hook; join with slip st to first sc.

Note: Loop a short piece of yarn around **back** of any stitch on Rnd 1 to mark **right** side.

Rnd 2: Ch 1, 2 sc in each sc around; join with slip st to first sc: 12 sc.

Rnd 3: Ch 1, 2 sc in same st, sc in next sc, (2 sc in next sc, sc in next sc) around; join with slip st to first sc: 18 sc.

Rnd 4: Ch 1, 2 sc in same st, sc in next 2 sc, (2 sc in next sc, sc in next 2 sc) around; join with slip st to first sc: 24 sc.

Rnd 5: Ch 1, 2 sc in same st, sc in next 3 sc, (2 sc in next sc, sc in next 3 sc) around; join with slip st to first sc: 30 sc.

Rnd 6: Ch 1, 2 sc in same st, sc in next 4 sc, (2 sc in next sc, sc in next 4 sc) around; join with slip st to first sc: 36 sc.

Rnd 7: Ch 1, 2 sc in same st, sc in next 5 sc, (2 sc in next sc, sc in next 5 sc) around; join with slip st to first sc: 42 sc.

Rnd 8: Ch 1, 2 sc in same st, sc in next 6 sc, (2 sc in next sc, sc in next 6 sc) around; join with slip st to first sc: 48 sc.

Rnd 9: Ch 1, 2 sc in same st, sc in next 7 sc, (2 sc in next sc, sc in next 7 sc) around; join with slip st to first sc: 54 sc.

Rnd 10: Ch 1, 2 sc in same st, sc in next 8 sc, (2 sc in next sc, sc in next 8 sc) around; join with slip st to first sc: 60 sc.

Rnd 11: Ch 1, 2 sc in same st, sc in next 9 sc, (2 sc in next sc, sc in next 9 sc) around; join with slip st to first sc: 66 sc.

Rnd 12: Ch 1, 2 sc in same st, sc in next 10 sc, (2 sc in next sc, sc in next 10 sc) around; join with slip st to first sc: 72 sc.

Rnd 13: Ch 1, 2 sc in same st, sc in next 11 sc, (2 sc in next sc, sc in next 11 sc) around; join with slip st to first sc: 78 sc.

Rnd 14: Ch 1, 2 sc in same st, sc in next 12 sc, (2 sc in next sc, sc in next 12 sc) around; join with slip st to first sc: 84 sc.

Rnd 15: Ch 1, 2 sc in same st, sc in next 13 sc, (2 sc in next sc, sc in next 13 sc) around; join with slip st to first sc: 84 sc.

Rnds 16-21: Ch 1, sc in same st and in each sc around; join with slip st to first sc.

Finish off.

PIE TOP

FILLING

Rnd 1 (Right side)**:** With Red, ch 2, 6 sc in second ch from hook; join with slip st to first sc.

Note: Mark last row as **right** side.

Rnd 2: Ch 1, 2 sc in each sc around; join with slip st to first sc: 12 sc.

Rnd 3: Ch 1, 2 sc in same st, sc in next sc, (2 sc in next sc, sc in next sc) around; join with slip st to first sc: 18 sc.

Rnd 4: Ch 1, 2 sc in same st, sc in next 2 sc, (2 sc in next sc, sc in next 2 sc) around; join with slip st to first sc: 24 sc.

Rnd 5: Ch 1, 2 sc in same st, sc in next 3 sc, (2 sc in next sc, sc in next 3 sc) around; join with slip st to first sc: 30 sc.

Rnd 6: Ch 1, 2 sc in same st, sc in next 4 sc, (2 sc in next sc, sc in next 4 sc) around; join with slip st to first sc: 36 sc.

Rnd 7: Ch 1, 2 sc in same st, sc in next 5 sc, (2 sc in next sc, sc in next 5 sc) around; join with slip st to first sc: 42 sc.

Rnd 8: Ch 1, 2 sc in same st, sc in next 6 sc, (2 sc in next sc, sc in next 6 sc) around; join with slip st to first sc: 48 sc.

Rnd 9: Ch 1, 2 sc in same st, sc in next 7 sc, (2 sc in next sc, sc in next 7 sc) around; join with slip st to first sc: 54 sc.

Rnd 10: Ch 1, 2 sc in same st, sc in next 8 sc, (2 sc in next sc, sc in next 8 sc) around; join with slip st to first sc: 60 sc.

Rnd 11: Ch 1, 2 sc in same st, sc in next 9 sc, (2 sc in next sc, sc in next 9 sc) around; join with slip st to first sc: 66 sc.

Rnd 12: Ch 1, 2 sc in same st, sc in next 10 sc, (2 sc in next sc, sc in next 10 sc) around; join with slip st to first sc: 72 sc.

Rnd 13: Ch 1, 2 sc in same st, sc in next 11 sc, (2 sc in next sc, sc in next 11 sc) around; join with slip st to first sc: 78 sc.

Rnd 14: Ch 1, 2 sc in same st, sc in next 12 sc, (2 sc in next sc, sc in next 12 sc) around; join with slip st to first sc: 84 sc.

Rnd 15: Ch 1, 2 sc in same st, sc in next 13 sc, (2 sc in next sc, sc in next 13 sc) around; join with slip st to first sc, finish off: 90 sc.

Instructions continued on page 38.

popcorn pillow

Movie popcorn is such an indulgence, but comfort shouldn't be. To that end, enjoy this movie-themed popcorn pillow. It's a good size to put behind your back while watching movies on the couch.

—Meagan

EASY

Finished Size: 6"w x 14½"h (15 cm x 37 cm)

MATERIALS

MEDIUM 4

Medium Weight Yarn
[7 ounces, 364 yards
(198 grams, 333 meters) per skein]:
- Red - 35 yards (32 meters)
- White - 35 yards (32 meters)
- Lt Yellow - 20 yards (18.5 meters)

Crochet hook, size K (6.5 mm) **or** size needed for gauge
Polyester fiberfill
Yarn needle

GAUGE: 10 sc and 11 rows = 4" (10 cm)

Gauge Swatch: 4" (10 cm) square
Ch 11.
Row 1: Sc in second ch from hook and in each ch across: 10 sc.
Rows 2-11: Ch 1, turn; sc in each sc across.
Finish off.

STITCH GUIDE

DECREASE
Pull up a loop in next 2 sts, YO and draw through all 3 loops on hook **(counts as one sc)**.

SIDE (Make 2)

With Red, ch 21.

Row 1 (Right side)**:** Sc in second ch from hook and in each ch across; finish off: 20 sc.

Note: Loop a short piece of yarn around any stitch to mark Row 1 as **right** side.

Row 2: With White, ch 6, sc in second ch from hook and in each ch across, with **wrong** side facing, sc in each sc across; finish off: 25 sc.

Row 3: With **right** side facing, join Red with sc in first sc *(see Joining With Sc, page 42)*; sc in each sc across; finish off.

Row 4: With White, ch 6, sc in second ch from hook and in each ch across, with **wrong** side facing, sc in each sc across; finish off: 30 sc.

Row 5: With **right** side facing, join Red with sc in first sc; sc in each sc across; finish off.

Row 6: With **wrong** side facing, join White with sc in first sc; sc in each sc across; finish off.

Rows 7-18: Repeat Rows 5 and 6, 6 times.

Row 19: With **right** side facing, join Red with sc in first sc; sc in next 24 sc, leave remaining 5 sc unworked; finish off: 25 sc.

Row 20: With **wrong** side facing, join White with sc in first sc; sc in each sc across; finish off.

Row 21: With **right** side facing, join Red with sc in first sc; sc in next 19 sc, leave remaining 5 sc unworked; finish off: 20 sc.

ASSEMBLY

With **wrong** sides together and working through **both** thicknesses, join White with slip st in first sc on Row 21; slip st in each st across; slip st in end of each row across to beginning ch; slip st in free loops of each ch across *(Fig. 2, page 42)*; leave remaining rows unworked; finish off.

POPCORN

Rnd 1: With **right** side facing and working in end of rows, join Lt Yellow with sc in first row; work 39 sc evenly spaced around; join with slip st to first sc: 40 sc.

Rnd 2: Ch 1, sc in same st and in each sc around; join with slip st to first sc.

Rnd 3: Ch 1, sc in same st and in next 2 sc, slip st in next sc, ch 4, ★ sc in next 3 sc, slip st in next sc, ch 4; repeat from ★ around; join with slip st to first sc.

Rnd 4: Ch 1, sc in same st and in next 2 sc, decrease, (sc in next 3 sc, decrease) around; join with slip st to first sc: 32 sc.

Rnd 5: Ch 1, sc in same st and in next 5 sc, decrease, (sc in next 6 sc, decrease) around; join with slip st to first sc: 28 sc.

Rnd 6: Ch 1, sc in same st and in next 2 sc, slip st in next sc, ch 4, ★ sc in next 3 sc, slip st in next sc, ch 4; repeat from ★ around; join with slip st to first sc.

Rnd 7: Ch 1, sc in same st and in next sc, decrease, (sc in next 2 sc, decrease) around; join with slip st to first sc: 21 sc.

Rnd 8: Ch 1, sc in same st and in next 2 sc, decrease, (sc in next 2 sc, decrease) around; join with slip st to first sc, finish off leaving a long end for sewing: 16 sc.

Stuff pillow with polyester fiberfill.

Whipstitch top seam *(Fig. 4, page 43)*.

Instructions continued on page 39.

computer virus pillow

Computer malfunctions drive me crazy, and I can't beat up my machine when it's misbehaving. Enter the computer virus: a menacing embodiment of everything that ails my computer, and a nicely smushable version, too. Hit it, squeeze it, and throw it across the room. It'll take the abuse and be ready for more—unlike your real computer, perhaps.

—Meagan

EASY

Finished Size: 6½"w x 8" h (including eyes) (16.5 cm x 20.5 cm)

MATERIALS
- Medium Weight Yarn (MEDIUM 4) [7 ounces, 364 yards (198 grams, 333 meters) per skein]:
  - Grey - 1 skein
  - Black - 15 yards (13.5 meters)
  - White - 5 yards (4.5 meters)
- Crochet hook, size J (6 mm) **or** size needed for gauge
- Polyester fiberfill
- Yarn needle

GAUGE: 11 sc and 13 rows = 4" (10 cm)

Gauge Swatch: 4" (10 cm) square
Ch 12.
Row 1: Sc in second ch from hook and in each ch across: 11 sc.
Rows 2-13: Ch 1, turn; sc in each sc across.
Finish off.

STITCH GUIDE

BEGINNING DECREASE

Pull up a loop in first 2 sts, YO and draw through all 3 loops on hook **(counts as one sc)**.

SCREEN

With Black, ch 16.

Row 1 (Right side)**:** Sc in second ch from hook and in each ch across: 15 sc.

Note: Loop a short piece of yarn around any stitch to mark Row 1 as **right** side.

Rows 2-17: Ch 1, turn; sc in each sc across.

Finish off.

SIDE (Make 5)

With Grey, ch 16.

Row 1 (Right side)**:** Sc in second ch from hook and in each ch across: 15 sc.

Note: Mark Row 1 as **right** side.

Rows 2-17: Ch 1, turn; sc in each sc across.

Finish off.

FRAME

BOTTOM EDGE

With Grey, ch 16.

Row 1: Sc in second ch from hook and in each ch across: 15 sc.

Row 2 (Right side)**:** Ch 1, turn; sc in each sc across; do **not** finish off.

Note: Mark Row 2 as **right** side.

FIRST SIDE EDGE

Row 1: Ch 1, turn; sc in first 2 sc, leave remaining 13 sc unworked: 2 sc.

Rows 3-12: Ch 1, turn; sc in each sc across.

Finish off.

SECOND SIDE EDGE

Row 1: With **wrong** side facing, skip next 11 sc and join Grey with sc in next sc *(see Joining With Sc, page 42)*, sc in last sc: 2 sc.

Rows 3-12: Ch 1, turn; sc in each sc across.

Finish off.

TOP EDGE

Row 1: With **wrong** side facing, join Grey with sc in first sc on First Side Edge; sc in next sc, ch 11 **loosely**, with **wrong** side of Second Side Edge facing, sc in first 2 sc: 4 sc and 11 chs.

Row 2: Ch 1, turn; sc in each sc and in each ch across: 15 sc.

Row 3: Ch 1, turn; sc in each sc across; finish off.

With **right** sides facing and Grey, using photo as a guide, sew Frame over Screen.

Instructions continued on page 39.

spiderweb hat

Ah, spiders. I love them for their creepiness, even though they scare the pants off me in real life. Confront your fears with this fun hat, which is especially perfect for chilly October weather. Or, for the more adventuresome, for year-round wear.

—Meagan

EASY

inished Size: Child{Small Adult-Adult}

Size Note: Instructions are written for size Child with sizes Small Adult and Adult in braces { }. Instructions will be easier to read if you circle all the numbers pertaining to your size. If only one number is given, it applies to all sizes.

MATERIALS

Medium Weight Yarn
[7 ounces, 364 yards
(198 grams, 333 meters) per skein]:
Black - 1 skein
White - 15{20-25} yards
[13.5{18.5-23} meters]
Crochet hook, size I (5.5 mm) **or** size needed for gauge
Yarn needle

GAUGE SWATCH: 4" (10 cm) diameter
Work Rnds 1-6 of Hat.

HAT

Rnd 1 (Wrong side)**:** With White, ch 2, 6 sc in second ch from hook; join with slip st to first sc, finish off.

Note: Loop a short piece of yarn around **back** of any stitch on Rnd 1 to mark **right** side.

Rnd 2: With **wrong** side facing, join Black with sc in same st as joining *(see Joining With Sc, page 42)*; sc in same st, 2 sc in each sc around; join with slip st to first sc: 12 sc.

Rnd 3: Ch 1, 2 sc in same st, sc in next sc, (2 sc in next sc, sc in next sc) around; join with slip st to first sc: 18 sc.

Rnd 4: Ch 1, 2 sc in same st, sc in next 2 sc, (2 sc in next sc, sc in next 2 sc) around; join with slip st to first sc, finish off: 24 sc.

Rnd 5: With **wrong** side facing, join White with sc in same st as joining; sc in same st and in next 3 sc, (2 sc in next sc, sc in next 3 sc) around; join with slip st to first sc, finish off: 30 sc.

Rnd 6: With **wrong** side facing, join Black with sc in same st as joining; sc in same st and in next 4 sc, (2 sc in next sc, sc in next 4 sc) around; join with slip st to first sc: 36 sc.

Rnd 7: Ch 1, 2 sc in same st, sc in next 5 sc, (2 sc in next sc, sc in next 5 sc) around; join with slip st to first sc, do **not** finish off: 42 sc.

Sizes Small Adult and Adult ONLY

Rnd 8: Ch 1, 2 sc in same st, sc in next 6 sc, (2 sc in next sc, sc in next 6 sc) around; join with slip st to first sc, finish off: 48 sc.

Rnd 9: With **wrong** side facing, join White with sc in same st as joining; sc in same st and in next 7 sc, (2 sc in next sc, sc in next 7 sc) around; join with slip st to first sc, finish off: 54 sc.

Size Adult ONLY

Rnd 10: With **wrong** side facing, join Black with sc in same st as joining; sc in same st and in next 8 sc, (2 sc in next sc, sc in next 8 sc) around; join with slip st to first sc: 60 sc.

Rnd 11: Ch 1, 2 sc in same st, sc in next 9 sc, (2 sc in next sc, sc in next 9 sc) around; join with slip st to first sc, do **not** finish off: 66 sc.

All Sizes

Continue working 3 rnds of Black and one rnd of White.

Rnds 8{10-12} thru 16{18-22}: Ch 1, sc in each sc around; join with slip st to first sc.

Finish off.

WEB PIECE (Make 6)

With White, make a chain long enough to go from outer edge to Rnd 1.

Using photo as a guide, sew Web pieces to Hat.

hamburger hat

I admit, I love the look of food. But when your head is cold and your belly is full, you can still enjoy a hamburger with this fun hat. It also makes a lovely pillow if you sew on a bottom and stuff it.

—Meagan

Finished Size: Child{Small Adult-Adult}

Size Note: Instructions are written for size Child with sizes Small Adult and Adult in braces { }. Instructions will be easier to read if you circle all the numbers pertaining to your size. If only one number is given, it applies to all sizes.

EASY

MATERIALS

MEDIUM 4

Medium Weight Yarn
[7 ounces, 364 yards
(198 grams, 333 meters) per skein]:
Tan - 1 skein
Black - 10{15-20} yards
[9{13.5-18.5} meters]
Green - 10{15-20} yards
[9{13.5-18.5} meters]
Red - 9{12-17} yards [8{11-15.5} meters]
Small Adult-Adult only
Yellow - {12-17} yards
[{11-15.5} meters]
Crochet hook, size I (5.5 mm) **or** size needed for gauge
Yarn needle

GAUGE: Rnds 1-6 = 4" (10 cm)

Gauge Swatch: 4" (10 cm) diameter
Work Rnds 1-6 of Hat.

HAT

Rnd 1 (Wrong side)**:** With Tan, ch 2, 6 sc in second ch from hook; join with slip st to first sc.

Note: Loop a short piece of yarn around **back** of any stitch on Rnd 1 to mark **right** side.

Rnd 2: Ch 1, 2 sc in each sc around; join with slip st to first sc: 12 sc.

Rnd 3: Ch 1, 2 sc in same st, sc in next sc, (2 sc in next sc, sc in next sc) around; join with slip st to first sc: 18 sc.

Rnd 4: Ch 1, 2 sc in same st, sc in next 2 sc, (2 sc in next sc, sc in next 2 sc) around; join with slip st to first sc: 24 sc.

Rnd 5: Ch 1, 2 sc in same st, sc in next 3 sc, (2 sc in next sc, sc in next 3 sc) around; join with slip st to first sc: 30 sc.

Rnd 6: Ch 1, 2 sc in same st, sc in next 4 sc, (2 sc in next sc, sc in next 4 sc) around; join with slip st to first sc: 36 sc.

Rnd 7: Ch 1, 2 sc in same st, sc in next 5 sc, (2 sc in next sc, sc in next 5 sc) around; join with slip st to first sc; do **not** finish off: 42 sc.

Sizes Small Adult and Adult ONLY

Rnd 8: Ch 1, 2 sc in same st, sc in next 6 sc, (2 sc in next sc, sc in next 6 sc) around; join with slip st to first sc: 48 sc.

Rnd 9: Ch 1, 2 sc in same st, sc in next 7 sc, (2 sc in next sc, sc in next 7 sc) around; join with slip st to first sc, do **not** finish off: 54 sc.

Sizes Child and Small Adult ONLY

Rnds 8{10} thru 10{12}: Ch 1, sc in same st and in each sc around; join with slip st to first sc: 42{54} sc.

Finish off.

Rnd 11{13}: With **wrong** side facing, join Green with sc in same st as joining ***(see Joining With Sc, page 42)***; sc in each sc around; join with slip st to first sc, finish off.

Rnd 12{14}: With **wrong** side facing, join Red with sc in same st as joining; sc in each sc around; join with slip st to first sc, finish off.

Size Child ONLY

Rnd 13: With **wrong** side facing, join Black with sc in same st as joining; sc in each sc around; join with slip st to first sc.

Rnd 14: Ch 1, sc in same st and in each sc around; join with slip st to first sc, finish off.

Rnd 15: With **wrong** side facing, join Tan with sc in same st as joining; sc in each sc around; join with slip st to first sc.

Rnd 16: Ch 1, sc in same st and in each sc around; join with slip st to first sc, finish off.

Size Small Adult ONLY

Rnd 15: With **wrong** side facing, join Yellow with sc in same st as joining; sc in each sc around; join with slip st to first sc, finish off.

Rnd 16: With **wrong** side facing, join Black with sc in same st as joining; sc in each sc around; join with slip st to first sc.

Rnds 17 and 18: Ch 1, sc in same st and in each sc around; join with slip st to first sc.

Finish off.

Rnd 19: With **wrong** side facing, join Tan with sc in same st as joining; sc in each sc around; join with slip st to first sc.

Rnd 20: Ch 1, sc in same st and in each sc around; join with slip st to first sc, finish off.

Size Adult ONLY

Rnd 10: Ch 1, 2 sc in same st, sc in next 8 sc, (2 sc in next sc, sc in next 8 sc) around; join with slip st to first sc, finish off: 60 sc.

Rnd 11: Ch 1, 2 sc in same st, sc in next 9 sc, (2 sc in next sc, sc in next 9 sc) around; join with slip st to first sc, finish off: 66 sc.

Rnds 12-14: Ch 1, sc in each sc around; join with slip st to first sc.

Finish off.

Rnd 15: With **wrong** side facing, join Green with sc in same st as joining; sc in each sc around; join with slip st to first sc.

Instructions continued on page 40.

birthday cake hat

This is another pattern that I put together as a basic canvas to decorate. Want more candles, different colored candles? Want to add a border of contrasting colo trim to the cake? Want to add crocheted flowers and leaves, embroidered lettering on the top of the cake, sequins and beads and other cake "confetti?" You can do a much to this cake as you can to a real one, with fewer calories and much longer lasting results. You can even add a bottom and stuff it for a cake centerpiece to us year after year.

—Meaga

EASY

Finished Size: Child{Small Adult- Adult}

Size Note: Instructions are written for size Child with sizes Small Adult and Adult in braces { }. Instructions will be easier to read if you circle all the numbers pertaining to your size. If only one number is given, it applies to all sizes.

MATERIALS

Medium Weight Yarn (MEDIUM 4)
[7 ounces, 364 yards (198 grams, 333 meters) per skein]:
- White - 1 skein
- Blue and Yellow - small amount **each**

Crochet hook, size I (5.5 mm) **or** size needed for gauge
Yarn needle
Wire (optional)

GAUGE: Rnds 1-6 = 4" (10 cm)

Gauge Swatch: 4" (10 cm) diameter
Work Rnds 1-6 of Hat.

HAT

Rnd 1 (Wrong side)**:** With White, ch 2, 6 sc in second ch from hook; join with slip st to first sc.

Note: Loop a short piece of yarn around **back** of any stitch on Rnd 1 to mark **right** side.

Rnd 2: Ch 1, 2 sc in each sc around; join with slip st to first sc: 12 sc.

Rnd 3: Ch 1, 2 sc in same st, sc in next sc, (2 sc in next sc, sc in next sc) around; join with slip st to first sc: 18 sc.

Rnd 4: Ch 1, 2 sc in same st, sc in next 2 sc, (2 sc in next sc, sc in next 2 sc) around; join with slip st to first sc: 24 sc.

Rnd 5: Ch 1, 2 sc in same st, sc in next 3 sc, (2 sc in next sc, sc in next 3 sc) around; join with slip st to first sc: 30 sc.

Rnd 6: Ch 1, 2 sc in same st, sc in next 4 sc, (2 sc in next sc, sc in next 4 sc) around; join with slip st to first sc; do **not** finish off: 36 sc.

Size Child ONLY
Rnd 7: Ch 1, 2 sc in same st, sc in next 5 sc, (2 sc in next sc, sc in next 5 sc) around; join with slip st to Front Loop Only of first sc *(Fig. 1, page 42)*, do **not** finish off: 42 sc.

Sizes Small Adult and Adult ONLY
Rnd 7: Ch 1, 2 sc in same st, sc in next 5 sc, (2 sc in next sc, sc in next 5 sc) around; join with slip st to first sc: 42 sc.

Rnd 8: Ch 1, 2 sc in same st, sc in next 6 sc, (2 sc in next sc, sc in next 6 sc) around; join with slip st to first sc, do **not** finish off: 48 sc.

Size Small Adult ONLY
Rnd 9: Ch 1, 2 sc in same st, sc in next 7 sc, (2 sc in next sc, sc in next 7 sc) around; join with slip st to Front Loop Only of first sc *(Fig. 1, page 42)*, do **not** finish off: 54 sc.

Size Adult ONLY
Rnd 9: Ch 1, 2 sc in same st, sc in next 7 sc, (2 sc in next sc, sc in next 7 sc) around; join with slip st to first sc: 54 sc.

Rnd 10: Ch 1, 2 sc in same st, sc in next 8 sc, (2 sc in next sc, sc in next 8 sc) around; join with slip st to first sc, finish off: 60 sc.

Rnd 11: Ch 1, 2 sc in same st, sc in next 9 sc, (2 sc in next sc, sc in next 9 sc) around; join with slip st to Front Loop Only of first sc *(Fig. 1, page 42)*, do **not** finish off: 66 sc.

All Sizes
Rnd 8{10-12}: Ch 1, working in Front Loop Only, sc in same st and in each sc around; join with slip st to **both** loops of first sc.

Rnds 9{11-13} thru 17{20-24}: Ch 1, sc in same st and in each sc around; join with slip st to first sc.

Instructions continued on page 40.

crown hat

Everybody should feel like royalty sometime. Wear this bold chapeau and you're declaring yourself king for a day—as well as keeping yourself nice and warm.

—Meagan

EASY

Finished Size: Child{Small Adult-Adult}

Size Note: Instructions are written for size Child with sizes Small Adult and Adult in braces { }. Instructions will be easier to read if you circle all the numbers pertaining to your size. If only one number is given, it applies to all sizes.

MATERIALS

MEDIUM 4

Medium Weight Yarn
[7 ounces, 364 yards
(198 grams, 333 meters) per skein]:
Purple - 75 yards (68.5 meters)
Yellow - 35 yards (32 meters)
White - 15 yards (13.5 meters)
Crochet hook, size I (5.5 mm) **or** size needed for gauge
Yarn needle

GAUGE: Rnds 1-6 = 4" (10 cm)

Gauge Swatch: 4" (10 cm) diameter
Work Rnds 1-6 of Hat.

BODY

Rnd 1 (Wrong side)**:** With Purple, ch 2, 6 sc in second ch from hook; join with slip st to first sc.

Note: Loop a short piece of yarn around **back** of any stitch on Rnd 1 to mark **right** side.

Rnd 2: Ch 1, 2 sc in each sc around; join with slip st to first sc: 12 sc.

Rnd 3: Ch 1, 2 sc in same st, sc in next sc, (2 sc in next sc, sc in next sc) around; join with slip st to first sc: 18 sc.

Rnd 4: Ch 1, 2 sc in same st, sc in next 2 sc, (2 sc in next sc, sc in next 2 sc) around; join with slip st to first sc: 24 sc.

Rnd 5: Ch 1, 2 sc in same st, sc in next 3 sc, (2 sc in next sc, sc in next 3 sc) around; join with slip st to first sc: 30 sc.

Rnd 6: Ch 1, 2 sc in same st, sc in next 4 sc, (2 sc in next sc, sc in next 4 sc) around; join with slip st to first sc: 36 sc.

Rnd 7: Ch 1, 2 sc in same st, sc in next 5 sc, (2 sc in next sc, sc in next 5 sc) around; join with slip st to first sc; do **not** finish off: 42 sc.

Sizes Small Adult and Adult ONLY
Rnd 8: Ch 1, 2 sc in same st, sc in next 6 sc, (2 sc in next sc, sc in next 6 sc) around; join with slip st to first sc: 48 sc.

Rnd 9: Ch 1, 2 sc in same st, sc in next 7 sc, (2 sc in next sc, sc in next 7 sc) around; join with slip st to first sc; do **not** finish off: 54 sc.

Size Adult ONLY
Rnd 10: Ch 1, 2 sc in same st, sc in next 8 sc, (2 sc in next sc, sc in next 8 sc) around; join with slip st to first sc: 60 sc.

Rnd 11: Ch 1, 2 sc in same st, sc in next 9 sc, (2 sc in next sc, sc in next 9 sc) around; join with slip st to first sc; do **not** finish off: 66 sc.

All Sizes
Rnds 8{10-12} thru 17{24-26}: Ch 1, sc in same st and in each sc around; join with slip st to first sc.

Finish off.

CROWN

Rnd 1: With **wrong** side facing, join Yellow with sc in same st as joining *(see Joining With Sc, page 42)*; sc in each sc around; join with slip st to first sc.

Rnds 2 thru 4{5-5}: Ch 1, sc in same st and in each sc around; join with slip st to first sc; do **not** finish off.

FIRST POINT

Row 1: Ch 1, sc in same st and in next 4{5-6} sc, leave remaining sc unworked: 5{6-7} sc.

Rows 2-4: Ch 1, turn; sc in each sc across.

Finish off.

REMAINING 5 POINTS

Row 1: With **right** side facing, skip next 2{3-4} sc from previous point and join Yellow with sc in next sc; sc in next 4{5-6} sc, leave remaining sc unworked: 5{6-7} sc.

Rows 2-4: Ch 1, turn; sc in each sc across.

Finish off.

Fold Crown to **right** side along Rnd 1 of Crown.

TRIM

Rnd 1: With **wrong** side facing and working through both thicknesses along fold, join White with sc in any sc; sc in each sc around; join with slip st to Back Loop Only of first sc *(Fig. 1, page 42)*.

Rnd 2: Ch 1, sc in Back Loops Only of same st and each sc around; join with slip st to **both** loops of first sc, finish off.

Tack Points in place.

Snake Scarf

continued from page 3.

TAIL

Row 1: Ch 1, turn; sc in each sc across to last 2 sc, decrease: 8 sc.

Row 2: Ch 1, turn; sc in each sc across.

Rows 3-12: Repeat Rows 1 and 2, 5 times: 3 sc.

Row 13: Ch 1, turn; sc in first sc, decrease: 2 sc.

Row 14: Ch 1, turn; sc in each sc across.

Row 15: Ch 1, turn; work beginning decrease; finish off.

EYE (Make 2)

Rnd 1 (Right side)**:** With Black, ch 2, 6 sc in second ch from hook; join with slip st to first sc, finish off.

Note: Mark Rnd 1 as **right** side.

Rnd 2: With **right** side facing, join Yellow with sc in same st as joining; 3 sc in same st, 2 sc in each of next 2 sc, 4 sc in next sc, 2 sc in each of last 2 sc; join with slip st to first sc, finish off.

Using photo as a guide, with **right** side facing, sew Eyes to Head.

Pie Pillow

continued from page 25.

LATTICE CRUST

LONG PIECE (Make 2)

With Gold, ch 5.

Row 1 (Right side)**:** Sc in second ch from hook and in each ch across: 4 sc.

Note: Mark Row 1 as **right** side.

Rows 2-35: Ch 1, turn; sc in each sc across.

Finish off.

MEDIUM PIECE (Make 4)

With Gold, ch 5.

Row 1 (Right side)**:** Sc in second ch from hook and in each ch across: 4 sc.

Note: Mark Row 1 as **right** side.

Rows 2-31: Ch 1, turn; sc in each sc across.

Finish off.

SHORT PIECE (Make 4)

With Gold, ch 5.

Row 1 (Right side)**:** Sc in second ch from hook and in each ch across: 4 sc.

Note: Mark Row 1 as **right** side.

Rows 2-27: Ch 1, turn; sc in each sc across.

Finish off.

FINISHING

Lay Lattice pieces over Pie Filling, Crossing the two Long Pieces over the middle, forming four quarter pie pieces. Lay two Middle Pieces on each side of each of the Long Pieces. Lay two Small Pieces on each side of the Medium Pieces. Using photo as a guide and beginning on one side of the Pie Filling, weave the pieces over and under the pieces to form the Lattice Crust spacing evenly and allowing the Pie Filling to show through. Pin Lattice Pieces in place to Pie Filling.

TRIM

Place the Pie Filling on the Bottom Crust with **wrong** sides together.
Working through **all** thicknesses, join Gold with sc in any st *(see Joining With Sc, page 42)*; sc in next sc, hdc in next 2 sc, (sc in next 2 sc, hdc in next 2 sc) around stuffing with polyester fiberfill before closing; join with slip st to first sc, finish off.

Popcorn Pillow

continued from page 27.

LABEL

With White, ch 14.

Row 1 (Right side)**:** Sc in second ch from hook and in each ch across: 13 sc.

Note: Mark Row 1 as **right** side.

Rows 2-5: Ch 1, turn; sc in each sc across.

Finish off.

Using photo below as a guide and **right** side facing. With Red and using straight stitch *(Fig. 5, page 43)*, add the word "POPCORN" to Label.

Sew Label to front of pillow.

Computer Virus Pillow

continued from page 29.

TOOTH (Make 4)

With White, ch 4.

Row 1: Sc in second ch from hook and in each ch across: 3 sc.

Row 2 (Right side)**:** Ch 1, turn; work beginning decrease, sc in last sc: 2 sc.

Note: Mark Row 2 as **right** side.

Row 3: Ch 1, turn; work beginning decrease: one st.

Row 4: Ch 1, turn; sc in sc; finish off.

With **right** sides facing and White, using photo as a guide, sew Teeth to Screen along inside edge of Frame.

Sew Sides and Screen together to form a cube, stuffing with polyester fiberfill before closing.

EYE (Make 2)

FRONT

Row 1 (Right side)**:** With Black, ch 2, 3 sc in second ch from hook; finish off.

Note: Mark Row 1 as **right** side.

Row 2: With **wrong** side facing, join White with sc in first sc; sc in same st, 2 sc in each of last 2 sc: 6 sc.

Row 3: Ch 1, turn; 2 sc in first sc, sc in next sc, (2 sc in next sc, sc in next sc) twice; finish off: 9 sc.

BACK

Row 1 (Right side)**:** With Grey, ch 2, 3 sc in second ch from hook.

Note: Mark Row 1 as **right** side.

Row 2: Ch 1, turn; 2 sc in each of first 3 sc: 6 sc.

Row 3: Ch 1, turn; 2 sc in first sc, sc in next sc, (2 sc in next sc, sc in next sc) twice; do **not** finish off: 9 sc.

Joining: With **wrong** sides of Front and Back together, Front facing, ch 1, sc evenly around entire piece; join with slip st to first sc, finish off.

Using photo as a guide, sew Eyes to top of pillow.

Hamburger Hat

continued from page 33.

Rnd 16: Ch 1, sc in same st and in each sc around; join with slip st to first sc; finish off.

Rnd 17: With **wrong** side facing, join Red with sc in same st as joining; sc in each sc around; join with slip st to first sc.

Rnd 18: Ch 1, sc in same st and in each sc around; join with slip st to first sc, finish off.

Rnd 19: With **wrong** side facing, join Yellow with sc in same st as joining; sc in each sc around; join with slip st to first sc.

Rnd 20: Ch 1, sc in same st and in each sc around; join with slip st to first sc, finish off.

Rnd 21: With **wrong** side facing, join Black with sc in same st as joining; sc in each sc around; join with slip st to first sc.

Rnds 22 and 23: Ch 1, sc in same st and in each sc around; join with slip st to first sc.

Finish off.

Rnd 24: With **wrong** side facing, join Tan with sc in same st as joining; sc in each sc around; join with slip st to first sc.

Rnds 25 and 26: Ch 1, sc in same st and in each sc around; join with slip st to first sc.

Finish off.

ALL SIZES

TOMATO SLICE (Make 3)

With Red, ch 11.

Row 1 (Right side)**:** Sc in second ch from hook in each ch across: 10 sc.

Note: Mark Row 1 as **right** side.

Row 2: Ch 1, turn; 2 sc in each sc across; finish off: 20 sc.

LETTUCE (Make 3)

With Green, ch 22.

Row 1 (Right side)**:** 2 Sc in second ch from hook, decrease, (2 sc in next sc, decrease) across; finish off: 14 sc.

Note: Mark Row 1 as **right** side.

Using photo as a guide, sew Tomato Slices and Lettuce to Hat.

Birthday Cake Hat

continued from page 35.

Rnd 18{21-25}: Ch 1, YO 3 times, insert hook in same st, YO and pull up a loop, YO and draw though all 5 loops on hook, ★ YO 3 times, insert hook in next sc, YO and pull up a loop, YO and draw though all 5 loops on hook; repeat from ★ around; join with slip st to first st, finish off.

CANDLE (Make 3)

With Blue, ch 6.

Row 1 (Right side)**:** Sc in second ch from hook and in each ch across; finish off: 5 sc.

Note: Mark Row 1 as **right** side.

FLAME

Row 1: With **right** side facing, join Yellow with sc to end of first sc *(see Joining With Sc, page 42)*: one sc.

Row 2: Ch 1, turn; sc in sc.

Row 3: Ch 1, turn; slip st in sc; finish off.

Optional: Run a piece of wire through Candle to straighten.

Using photo as a guide, sew Candles to top of Hat.

TIP: Easy-to-memorize patterns let you multitask, crocheting during movies and phone calls.

GENERAL INSTRUCTIONS

ABBREVIATIONS

ch(s)	chain(s)
cm	centimeters
dc	double crochet(s)
hdc	half double crochet(s)
mm	millimeters
sc	single crochet(s)
st(s)	stitch(es)
tr	treble crochet(s)
YO	yarn over

★ — work instructions following ★ as many **more** times as indicated in addition to the first time.

† to † **or** ♥ to ♥ — work all instructions from first † to second † **or** first ♥ to second ♥ **as many** times as specified.

( ) or [ ] — work enclosed instructions **as many** times as specified by the number immediately following **or** work all enclosed instructions in the stitch or space indicated **or** contains explanatory remarks.

colon (:) — the number(s) given after a colon at the end of a row or round denote(s) the number of stitches you should have on that row or round.

CROCHET TERMINOLOGY		
UNITED STATES		INTERNATIONAL
slip stitch (slip st)	=	single crochet (sc)
single crochet (sc)	=	double crochet (dc)
half double crochet (hdc)	=	half treble crochet (htr)
double crochet (dc)	=	treble crochet(tr)
treble crochet (tr)	=	double treble crochet (dtr)
double treble crochet (dtr)	=	triple treble crochet (ttr)
triple treble crochet (tr tr)	=	quadruple treble crochet (qtr)
skip	=	miss

GAUGE

Exact gauge is **essential** for proper size. Before beginning your project, make the sample swatch given in the individual instructions in the yarn and hook specified. After completing the swatch, measure it, counting your stitches and rows or rounds carefully. If your swatch is larger or smaller than specified, **make another, changing hook size to get the correct gauge**. Keep trying until you find the size hook that will give you the specified gauge.

Yarn Weight Symbol & Names	LACE 0	SUPER FINE 1	FINE 2	LIGHT 3	MEDIUM 4	BULKY 5	SUPER BULKY 6
Type of Yarns in Category	Fingering, 10-count crochet thread	Sock, Fingering Baby	Sport, Baby	DK, Light Worsted	Worsted, Afghan, Aran	Chunky, Craft, Rug	Bulky, Roving
Crochet Gauge* Ranges in Single Crochet to 4" (10 cm)	32-42 double crochets**	21-32 sts	16-20 sts	12-17 sts	11-14 sts	8-11 sts	5-9 sts
Advised Hook Size Range	Steel*** 6,7,8 Regular hook B-1	B-1 to E-4	E-4 to 7	7 to I-9	I-9 to K-10.5	K-10.5 to M-13	M-13 and larger

*GUIDELINES ONLY: The chart above reflects the most commonly used gauges and hook sizes for specific yarn categories.

** Lace weight yarns are usually crocheted on larger-size hooks to create lacy openwork patterns. Accordingly, a gauge range is difficult to determine. Always follow the gauge stated in your pattern.

*** Steel crochet hooks are sized differently from regular hooks–the higher the number the smaller the hook, which is the reverse of regular hook sizing.

CROCHET HOOKS													
U.S.	B-1	C-2	D-3	E-4	F-5	G-6	H-8	I-9	J-10	K-10½	N	P	Q
Metric - mm	2.25	2.75	3.25	3.5	3.75	4	5	5.5	6	6.5	9	10	15

BEGINNER	Projects for first-time crocheters using basic stitches. Minimal shaping.
EASY	Projects using yarn with basic stitches, repetitive stitch patterns, simple color changes, and simple shaping and finishing.
INTERMEDIATE	Projects using a variety of techniques, such as basic lace patterns or color patterns, mid-level shaping and finishing.
EXPERIENCED	Projects with intricate stitch patterns, techniques and dimension, such as non-repeating patterns, multi-color techniques, fine threads, small hooks, detailed shaping and refined finishing.

JOINING WITH SC

When instructed to join with sc, begin with a slip knot on hook. Insert hook in stitch or space indicated, YO and pull up a loop, YO and draw through both loops on hook.

BACK OR FRONT LOOP ONLY

Work only in loop(s) indicated by arrow *(Fig. 1)*.

Fig. 1

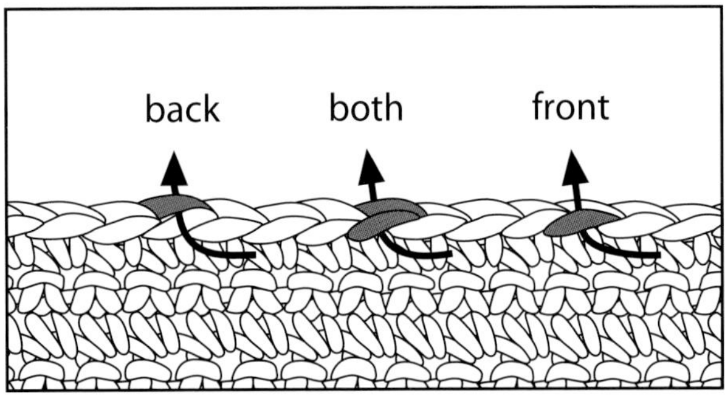

FREE LOOPS OF A CHAIN

When instructed to work in free loops of a chain, work in loop indicated by arrow *(Fig. 2)*.

Fig. 2

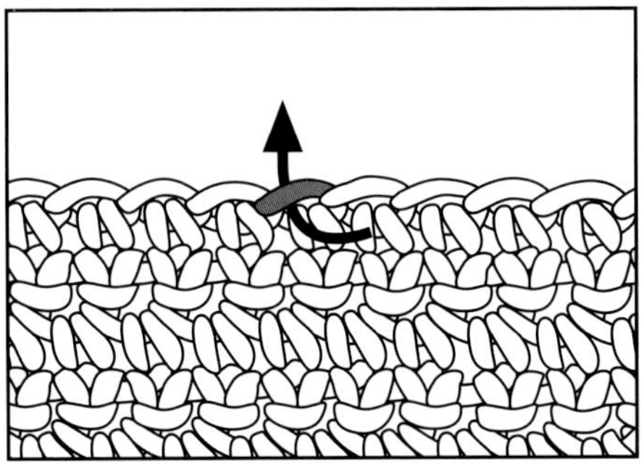

CHANGING COLORS

Insert hook in stitch indicated, YO and pull up a loop, drop yarn, with new yarn ***(Fig. 3a)***, YO and draw through both loops on hook. Working over yarn when instructed ***(Fig. 3b)***.

Fig. 3a

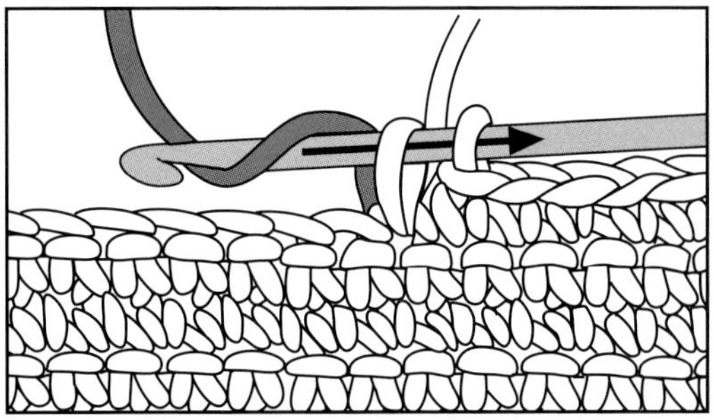

Fig. 3b

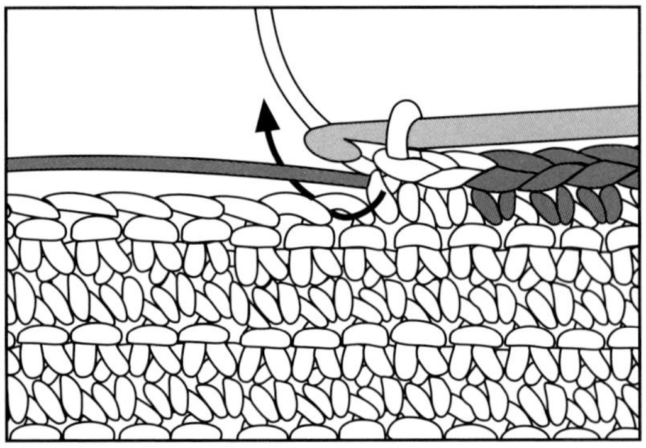

WHIPSTITCH

Place two pieces with **wrong** sides together. Sew through both pieces once to secure the beginning of the seam, leaving an ample yarn end to weave in later.Insert the needle from **back** to **front** through **both** loops on **both** pieces (Fig. 4). Bring the needle around and insert it from **back** to **front** through next loops of both pieces. Continue in this manner across, keeping the sewing yarn fairly loose.

Fig. 4

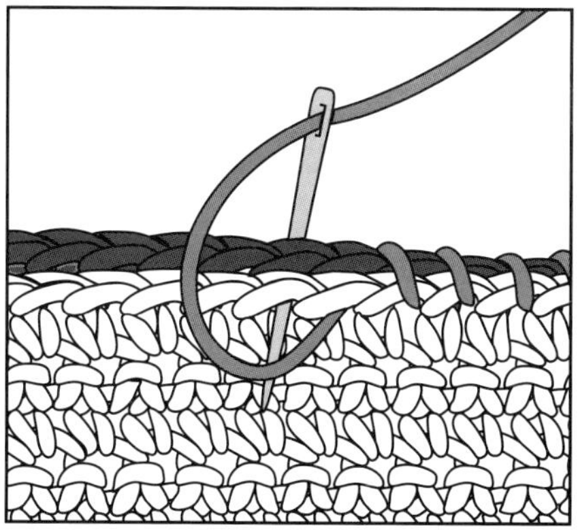

STRAIGHT STITCH

Straight stitch is just what the name implies, a single, straight stitch. Come up at 1 and go down at 2 *(Fig. 5)*.

Fig. 5

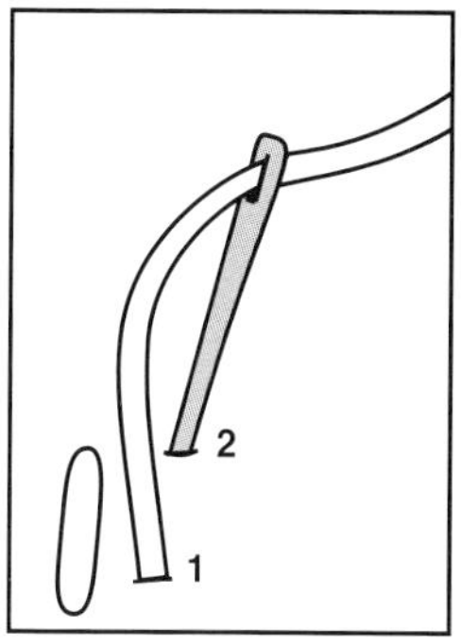

We have made every effort to ensure that these instructions are accurate and complete. We cannot, however, be responsible for human error, typographical mistakes, or variations in individual work.

Production Team: Instructional Editor - Lois J. Long; Technical Editor - Sarah J. Green; Editorial Writer - Susan McManus Johnson; Senior Graphic Artist - Lora Puls; Graphic Artist - Dana Vaughn; Photo Stylist - Sondra Daniel; and Photographer - Ken West.

YARN INFORMATION

Each project in this leaflet was made using Red Heart® Super Saver®. Any brand of Medium Weight Yarn may be used. It is best to refer to the yardage/meters when determining how many balls or skeins to purchase. Remember, to arrive at the finished size, it is the GAUGE/TENSION that is important, not the brand of yarn.

For your convenience, listed below are the specific colors used to create our photography models.

SNAKE SCARF
Purple - #776 Dk Orchid
Green - #389 Hunter Green
Yellow - #324 Bright Yellow
Black - #312 Black

ROAD SCARF
Yellow - #324 Bright Yellow
Black - #312 Black
White - #311 White

PENCIL SCARF
Gold - #321 Gold
Black - #312 Black
Pink - #372 Rose Pink
Grey - #400 Grey Heather
Tan - #334 Buff

DIAMOND ILLUSION SCARF
Black - #312 Black
White - #311 White

TIC-TAC-TOAST
Tan - #334 Buff
White - #311 White
Yellow - #324 Bright Yellow
Dk Red - #376 Burgundy
Red - #319 Cherry Red

SMILEY FACE AFGHAN SQUARE
Yellow - #324 Bright Yellow
Black - #312 Black

PEACE SIGN AFGHAN SQUARE
Black - #312 Black
White - #311 White

YIN-YANG AFGHAN SQUARE
Black - #312 Black
White - #311 White

TRAFFIC LIGHT PILLOW
Black - #312 Black
Yellow - #324 Bright Yellow
Red - #319 Cherry Red
Green - #672 Spring Green

BEAKER PILLOW
Green - #672 Spring Green
Grey - #400 Grey Heather

FORTUNE COOKIE PILLOW
Tan - #334 Buff
White - #311 White

MOODY PILLOW
Yellow - #324 Bright Yellow
Blue - #512 Turquoise
Black - #312 Black

PIE PILLOW
Gold - #320 Cornmeal
Red - #319 Cherry Red

POPCORN PILLOW
White - #311 White
Red - #319 Cherry Red
Lt Yellow - #322 Pale Yellow

COMPUTER VIRUS PILLOW
Grey - #341 Lt Grey
Black - #312 Black
White - #311 White

SPIDERWEB HAT
Black - #312 Black
White - #311 White

HAMBURGER HAT
Tan - #336 Warm Brown
Green - #672 Spring Green
Red - #319 Cherry Red
Yellow - #324 Bright Yellow
Black - #312 Black

BIRTHDAY CAKE HAT
White - #311 White
Blue - #512 Turquoise
Yellow - #324 Bright Yellow

CROWN HAT
Purple - #776 Dk Orchid
Yellow - #324 Bright Yellow
White - #311 White